WORKBOOK

For

The Armor of God - Bible Study Book with Video Access

A Guide To Priscilla Shirer's Book

Willow Reads

How To Use This Workbook

This workbook is designed to help you engage with the content of the original book in a meaningful and interactive way.

1. Start with the Overview
Begin your journey through this workbook by reading the "Overview of the Original Book." This section provides a concise summary of the key themes and concepts explored in the main book. It's the perfect starting point to refresh your memory or get acquainted with the book's content.

2. Dive into the Chapters
Each chapter in this workbook is dedicated to a corresponding chapter in the original book. Here's what you'll find in each chapter section:

Key Lessons:
Discover the fundamental takeaways from the main book's chapter. These key lessons will help you understand the core concepts discussed in that section.

Exercises:
Engage actively with the material through exercises that encourage reflection, application, and critical thinking.

These exercises will help you internalize and apply the book's teachings.

Questions:
Explore thought-provoking questions related to the chapter's content. Use these questions for personal reflection or as a basis for discussions with others who have read the original book.

Chapter Summary:
Get a quick recap of the chapter's main points. This summary will reinforce your understanding and serve as a handy reference.

3. Final Evaluation Questions
Towards the end of this workbook, you'll find a section titled "Final Evaluation Questions." This is your opportunity to test your knowledge and insights gained from the entire book. These questions will challenge you to think critically, make connections, and draw your own conclusions.

4. Your Journey, Your Pace
This workbook is designed to be flexible. You can use it in a way that suits your needs and preferences. Whether you want to complete it in a linear fashion, jump to specific chapters, or revisit sections for further reflection, it's entirely up to you.

Overview Of The Original Book

The Armor of God: A Bible Study Book with Video Access is a comprehensive study of Ephesians 6:10-17, which outlines the spiritual armor that God provides for Christians to protect them from the attacks of the enemy. This book is designed to help readers understand the significance of each piece of armor and how to apply it to their daily lives.

In The Armor of God, author Priscilla Shirer takes readers on a journey through the Scriptures to explore the depths of God's love and protection. She reveals the power of each piece of armor and how it can be used to stand firm against the enemy's temptations and attacks. This book is a valuable resource for anyone who wants to learn more about spiritual warfare and how to live a victorious Christian life.

The Armor of God is a metaphor for the spiritual protection that God provides for Christians. In Ephesians 6:10-17, the apostle Paul uses the analogy of a soldier's armor to describe the spiritual weapons that Christians need to protect themselves from the attacks of the enemy.

The six pieces of armor that Paul describes are:

- The belt of truth
- The breastplate of righteousness
- The shoes of the gospel of peace
- The shield of faith
- The helmet of salvation
- The sword of the Spirit

Each piece of armor has a specific purpose and corresponds to a specific aspect of spiritual warfare. For example, the belt of truth protects our minds from deception, while the breastplate of righteousness protects our hearts from sin.

How to Apply the Armor of God
In The Armor of God, Priscilla Shirer provides practical guidance on how to apply the armor of God to our daily lives. She encourages readers to put on the armor each day and to use it to stand firm against the enemy's temptations and attacks.

Here are some of the key takeaways from Shirer's teaching:

- The armor of God is not about self-effort; it is about relying on God's strength and power.

- We need to put on the armor of God every day, just as a soldier puts on his armor before going into battle.

- The armor of God is effective against all of the enemy's weapons.

- We need to use the armor of God in conjunction with prayer and the power of the Holy Spirit.

The Armor of God is a valuable resource for anyone who wants to learn more about spiritual warfare and how to live a victorious Christian life.

Table Of Contents

Sizing Up The Enemy

Chapter Summary

This section details the nature and tactics of the enemy, Satan, and his fallen angels. This understanding is crucial for equipping Christians with the knowledge and resolve to effectively utilize the armor of God in spiritual warfare.

The author begins by emphasizing the reality of Satan and his demonic forces, highlighting their existence as formidable adversaries. Satan is not a mere symbol or personification of evil but a powerful, intelligent being who actively opposes God's plan for humanity.

She then explores the tactics and strategies employed by Satan and his demons, emphasizing their deception, manipulation, and temptation. Satan seeks to sow doubt, twist perceptions, and entice individuals away from God's righteousness. He targets both the mind and the heart, exploiting weaknesses and vulnerabilities to lead people astray.

The author highlights the importance of recognizing the enemy's tactics, emphasizing that ignorance of their methods leaves us vulnerable to their attacks.

By understanding Satan's strategies, we can better discern his temptations and employ the armor of God effectively.

To further illustrate the enemy's cunning, the author provides examples from Scripture of individuals who fell prey to Satan's deception, such as Adam and Eve in the Garden of Eden and Ananias and Sapphira in the early church. These examples serve as cautionary tales, reminding us of the enemy's power and the need for vigilance.

She concludes by emphasizing the importance of not underestimating the enemy. While Satan and his demons are formidable foes, they are no match for God's power and the protection of the armor of God. Christians are called to be bold and courageous, standing firm against the enemy's attacks and wielding the armor of God with confidence.

Key Lessons

1. Satan and his demonic forces are real and active adversaries in spiritual warfare. They are not mere symbols or personifications of evil but powerful, intelligent beings who oppose God's plan for humanity.

2. Satan employs deception, manipulation, and temptation as his primary tactics. He seeks to sow doubt, twist perceptions, and entice individuals away from God's righteousness, targeting both the mind and the heart to exploit weaknesses and vulnerabilities.

3. Recognizing the enemy's tactics is crucial for effective spiritual warfare. Ignorance of their methods leaves us vulnerable to their attacks. Understanding Satan's strategies allows us to discern his temptations and employ the armor of God wisely.

4. While Satan and his demons are formidable foes, they are no match for God's power and the protection of the armor of God. Christians are called to be bold and courageous, standing firm against the enemy's attacks with confidence in God's unwavering protection.

Self-reflection questions

How has your understanding of Satan and his demonic forces impacted your perception of spiritual warfare? How do you view the role of spiritual warfare in your daily life?

_____

_____

_____

_____

_____

_____

_____

_____

_____

In what ways have you experienced the tactics of deception, manipulation, and temptation employed by Satan? How have you identified and resisted these temptations?

How can you cultivate a deeper awareness of the enemy's strategies, increasing your discernment and ability to recognize his attempts to influence your thoughts and actions?

_____

_____

_____

_____

_____

_____

Which areas of your life might be particularly vulnerable to Satan's attacks? How can you strengthen your defenses and seek God's protection in these areas?

_____

_____

_____

_____

_____

_____

_____

_____

_____

In what ways can you learn from the examples of individuals in Scripture who fell prey to Satan's deception? How can you avoid similar pitfalls?

_____

_____

_____

_____

_____

How can you maintain a balanced perspective on the enemy's power, recognizing their formidable nature while also affirming God's ultimate sovereignty and the strength of the armor of God?

How can you cultivate boldness and courage in the face of spiritual opposition? How can you draw upon God's strength and assurance to stand firm against the enemy's attacks?

_____

_____

_____

_____

_____

_____

_____

_____

Life-Changing Exercises

1. Engage in regular study of God's Word, specifically passages that address spiritual warfare and the armor of God. This will deepen your understanding of the enemy's tactics and strategies, empowering you to recognize and resist his temptations.

2. Cultivate a habit of prayer that includes specific requests for protection from spiritual attacks and

guidance in discerning the enemy's influence in your life. Prayer is a powerful weapon in spiritual warfare, and it allows you to tap into God's strength and wisdom.

3. Seek accountability and support from fellow believers who share your commitment to spiritual growth and warfare. Engage in regular conversations and prayer with trusted friends, mentors, or small group members, seeking guidance and encouragement in your spiritual battles.

4. Practice mindfulness and self-awareness, paying attention to your thoughts, emotions, and motivations. This will help you identify areas of vulnerability and recognize instances where the enemy might be attempting to influence your decisions and actions.

The Belt Of Truth

Chapter Summary

The author explores the significance of the first piece of armor, the belt of truth, and its role in spiritual warfare. Truth is presented as the foundation upon which all other pieces of armor are built, emphasizing its centrality in the Christian life.

She begins by defining truth as the accurate representation of reality, aligning with God's character and his revelation in Scripture. Truth is not merely a matter of personal opinion or subjective interpretation but an objective standard that reflects God's nature and his design for humanity.

She then highlights the importance of truth in spiritual warfare, emphasizing its power to dispel deception and protect from the enemy's lies. Satan, as the father of lies, seeks to distort truth, manipulate perceptions, and lead individuals astray. The belt of truth serves as a shield against these attacks, providing a secure foundation for discerning right from wrong and aligning with God's will.

The author emphasizes the significance of living a life of truthfulness, embodying honesty and integrity in all aspects of life. This includes aligning one's thoughts, words, and actions with God's truth, avoiding deception, hypocrisy, and self-deception. Living a truthful life not only strengthens our spiritual defenses but also reflects God's character and promotes trust in our relationships with others.

The author further explores the practical implications of the belt of truth, suggesting that it manifests in our daily lives through:

- Seeking truth in all things, including diligent study of Scripture and discernment in evaluating information.

- Speaking the truth with love, balancing honesty with compassion and sensitivity to others.

- Avoiding gossip, slander, and malicious speech, recognizing the destructive power of untruths.

- Confessing and repenting of sins, seeking forgiveness and cleansing from God and those we have wronged.

Key Lessons

1. Truth is the foundation upon which all other pieces of armor are built. Just as a belt secures and strengthens the rest of the armor, truth provides a stable foundation for spiritual warfare. It is essential for discernment, making wise decisions, and living a life aligned with God's will.

2. Satan, as the father of lies, seeks to distort truth and manipulate perceptions. He attacks the belt of truth through deception, hypocrisy, and self-deception. It is crucial to be vigilant against these attacks, seeking truth in all things and aligning our thoughts, words, and actions with God's revelation.

3. Living a life of truthfulness is not only a spiritual obligation but also a reflection of God's character. Embodying honesty and integrity in our daily interactions fosters trust in our relationships and strengthens our witness to the world.

4. The belt of truth manifests in practical ways, such as seeking truth in all things, speaking the truth with love, avoiding gossip and malicious speech, and confessing and repenting of sins. These actions not only protect us from spiritual

attacks but also contribute to a more just and loving world.

Self-reflection questions

How has your understanding of truth, as both an objective standard and a reflection of God's character, shaped your perspective on spiritual warfare?

_____

_____

_____

_____

_____

_____

_____

_____

In what ways have you experienced the enemy's attacks on your belt of truth, through deception, manipulation, or self-deception? How have you recognized and resisted these attacks?

_____

_____

_____

_____

_____

_____

_____

_____

How can you cultivate a deeper commitment to living a life of truthfulness, embodying honesty and integrity in all aspects of your life?

_____

_____

_____

_____

_____

_____

_____

_____

How can you be more diligent in examining the
information you consume, seeking truth from reliable
sources and discerning fact from fiction?

_____

_____

_____

_____

_____

_____

_____

_____

_____

_____

How can you balance speaking the truth with love,
ensuring that your honesty is delivered with compassion
and sensitivity to others?

_____

_____

_____

_____

_____

_____

How can you be more mindful of your speech, avoiding gossip, slander, and malicious words that can damage relationships and undermine the power of truth?

How can you cultivate a regular practice of confession and repentance, seeking forgiveness from God and those you have wronged, allowing truth to restore broken relationships and strengthen your spiritual foundation?

_____

_____

_____

_____

_____

_____

_____

Life-Changing Exercises

1. Commit to daily Bible study, immersing yourself in God's Word, the ultimate source of truth. Allow Scripture to shape your understanding of truth, guide your decision-making, and provide a foundation for discerning right from wrong.

2. Cultivate a habit of mindfulness and self-reflection, paying attention to your thoughts, words, and actions. Identify areas where you may compromise truth, whether through deception, hypocrisy, or self-deception. Seek God's guidance in addressing these areas and aligning your life with His truth.

3. Engage in regular conversations with trusted friends, mentors, or small group members, seeking feedback and encouragement in your pursuit of truthfulness. Share your struggles, seek advice, and hold each other accountable in living lives that reflect God's character.

4. Actively challenge your own biases and assumptions, seeking to understand different perspectives and consider alternative viewpoints. This openness to truth will help you break free from echo chambers and embrace a more comprehensive understanding of reality.

The Breastplate Of Righteousness

Chapter Summary

Righteousness is presented as the shield that guards against sin and the enemy's attacks on our moral purity.

This chapter defines righteousness as the state of being in right relationship with God, characterized by obedience to His laws and moral standards. It is not merely about external actions but about a heart that is aligned with God's will and seeks to live a holy life.

The author highlights the importance of the breastplate of righteousness in spiritual warfare, emphasizing its power to protect the heart, the seat of our emotions, thoughts, and intentions. The heart is a primary target of Satan's attacks, as it is the source of our actions and the foundation of our character. Righteousness serves as a shield, deflecting the enemy's attempts to corrupt our hearts and lead us astray from God's righteousness.

She emphasizes the transformative power of righteousness, highlighting its ability to cleanse our hearts from sin, renew our minds, and empower us to make wise decisions. As we put on the breastplate of righteousness, we experience the sanctifying work of the

Holy Spirit, who conforms us to the image of Christ and strengthens our commitment to holy living.

To effectively utilize the breastplate of righteousness, she suggests practical steps such as:

- Seeking God's righteousness through repentance and faith in Jesus Christ. This involves acknowledging our sinfulness, turning away from sin, and embracing Christ's forgiveness and righteousness as our own.

- Living according to God's standards, outlined in Scripture. This includes obeying His commandments, pursuing holiness in all aspects of life, and treating others with love, compassion, and justice.

- Abiding in God's Word and seeking His guidance in making decisions. Scripture provides a roadmap for righteous living, helping us discern right from wrong and navigate the complexities of life.

- Surrendering our hearts to God's control, allowing Him to transform our desires and motivations. This involves surrendering our will to God, seeking His guidance, and striving to align our thoughts, words, and actions with His righteousness.

Key Lessons

1. Righteousness is the state of being in right relationship with God, characterized by obedience to His laws and moral standards. It is not merely about external actions but about a heart that is aligned with God's will and seeks to live a holy life.

2. The breastplate of righteousness is crucial in spiritual warfare, protecting our hearts, the seat of our emotions, thoughts, and intentions. The heart is a primary target of Satan's attacks, and righteousness serves as a shield, deflecting his attempts to corrupt our hearts and lead us astray from God's righteousness.

3. Righteousness is not achieved through self-effort but through repentance and faith in Jesus Christ. By acknowledging our sinfulness, turning away from sin, and embracing Christ's forgiveness and righteousness as our own, we can experience the transformative power of God's righteousness.

4. Wearing the breastplate of righteousness involves living according to God's standards, outlined in Scripture, abiding in His Word, seeking His guidance in decision-making, and surrendering our hearts to His control. This allows us to stand firm in our commitment to God's righteousness, confident in His protection and guidance on the path of righteousness and holiness.

Self-reflection questions

How has your understanding of righteousness, both as a state of being and a gift from God, shaped your approach to spiritual warfare and your pursuit of holiness?

_____

_____

_____

_____

_____

_____

In what ways have you experienced the enemy's attacks on your moral purity, seeking to corrupt your heart and lead you astray from God's righteousness? How have you recognized and resisted these attacks?

_____

_____

_____

_____

_____

_____

_____

How can you cultivate a deeper commitment to seeking God's righteousness through repentance and faith in Jesus Christ, allowing His transformative power to shape your heart and guide your actions?

_____

_____

_____

_____

_____

_____

_____

_____

How can you diligently examine your actions, motivations, and desires, ensuring that they align with God's standards of righteousness, as outlined in Scripture?

_____

_____

_____

_____

_____

_____

_____

_____

How can you make God's Word your guiding principle,
seeking His wisdom and direction in making decisions,
both big and small?

_____

_____

_____

_____

_____

_____

_____

How can you surrender your heart to God's control, allowing Him to transform your thoughts, emotions, and motivations, bringing them into alignment with His perfect righteousness?

_____

_____

_____

_____

_____

_____

_____

How can you consistently seek accountability and support from trusted friends, mentors, or small group members, sharing your struggles and seeking encouragement in your pursuit of a righteous life?

_____

_____

_____

_____

_____

_____

_____

_____

Life-Changing Exercises

1. Engage in regular meditation on Scripture, specifically passages that emphasize God's righteousness and His call to holiness. This will deepen your understanding of righteousness and cultivate a desire to live a life that reflects God's character.

2. Practice daily examination of conscience, reflecting on your thoughts, words, and actions in light of God's standards. Identify areas where you have fallen short of righteousness and seek God's

forgiveness and guidance in making necessary changes.

3. Develop a habit of regular prayer, specifically seeking God's help in pursuing righteousness and resisting temptation. Prayer is a powerful tool that allows you to draw upon God's strength and wisdom in your spiritual journey.

4. Engage in intentional acts of service and compassion, seeking opportunities to reflect God's love and righteousness in your interactions with others. These acts not only bless others but also strengthen your own commitment to righteous living.

The Shoes Of Peace

Chapter Summary

Peace is presented as the bedrock upon which other pieces of armor stand, enabling stability and readiness to confront spiritual opposition.

The author begins by defining peace not merely as the absence of conflict but as a state of tranquility, harmony, and well-being that stems from a right relationship with God. True peace is not a product of external circumstances but a reflection of an inner state of being aligned with God's will.

She then highlights the importance of the shoes of peace in spiritual warfare, emphasizing their power to ground us in stability and enable us to stand firm against the enemy's attacks. The shoes of peace provide a secure footing, preventing us from being swayed by the enemy's tactics of fear, anxiety, and unrest.

She emphasizes the transformative power of peace, highlighting its ability to calm our hearts, quiet our minds, and empower us to make wise decisions in the face of adversity.

As we put on the shoes of peace, we experience the soothing presence of the Holy Spirit, who brings tranquility amidst chaos and strengthens our resolve to remain steadfast in our faith.

Key Lessons

1. Peace is not merely the absence of conflict but a state of tranquility, harmony, and well-being that stems from a right relationship with God. True peace is not a product of external circumstances but a reflection of an inner state of being aligned with God's will.

2. The shoes of peace are crucial in spiritual warfare, providing a firm foundation and enabling us to stand firm against the enemy's attacks. They prevent us from being swayed by the enemy's tactics of fear, anxiety, and unrest, allowing us to approach spiritual battles with stability and confidence.

3. Cultivating peace involves forgiveness, contentment, humility, and a positive outlook. Forgiveness allows us to release burdens and embrace inner peace, while contentment fosters gratitude for God's blessings and reduces attachment to worldly possessions. Humility

enables us to rely on God's strength and submit to His will, while a positive outlook counters the enemy's attempts to instill fear and doubt.

4. Wearing the shoes of peace provides stability and readiness in the face of spiritual opposition. It empowers us to face challenges with a calm heart and a clear mind, knowing that God's peace will guide us through trials and tribulations, enabling us to stand victorious in any spiritual battle.

Self-reflection questions

How has your understanding of peace, as both a gift from God and a state of being, shaped your approach to spiritual warfare and your pursuit of inner tranquility?

_____

_____

In what ways have you experienced the enemy's attempts
to disrupt your peace, sowing seeds of fear, anxiety, and
unrest? How have you recognized and resisted these
attacks?

_____

_____

_____

_____

_____

_____

_____

_____

How can you cultivate a deeper commitment to forgiveness and reconciliation, releasing resentments and extending grace to those who have wronged you, allowing peace to take root in your heart?

How can you cultivate a spirit of contentment and gratitude, appreciating God's blessings and gifts, both big and small, and finding joy in simplicity rather than chasing worldly possessions?

_____

_____

_____

_____

_____

_____

_____

How can you embrace humility and submission to God's will, acknowledging your limitations and seeking His guidance in all aspects of your life, trusting His sovereignty even in the face of challenges?

_____

_____

_____

_____

_____

_____

_____

How can you cultivate a positive and hopeful outlook, focusing on God's promises and the ultimate victory of His Kingdom, refusing to let the enemy's attempts to instill fear and doubt undermine your faith?

_____

_____

_____

_____

_____

_____

_____

_____

_____

_____

_____

How can you intentionally seek out opportunities to
promote peace and reconciliation in your relationships
with others, acting as a peacemaker and reflecting God's
peace in the world around you?

_____

_____

_____

_____

_____

_____

_____

_____

_____

_____

_____

Life-Changing Exercises

1. Engage in regular meditation on Scripture, specifically passages that emphasize God's peace and His promises of tranquility. This will deepen your understanding of peace and cultivate a desire to experience its transformative power in your life.

2. Practice daily journaling, reflecting on moments of peace and gratitude, as well as instances where you have experienced anxiety or unrest. This will help you identify patterns, recognize triggers, and develop strategies for cultivating peace in the midst of challenges.

3. Cultivate a habit of mindfulness, paying attention to your thoughts, emotions, and physical sensations, especially in moments of stress or conflict. This will allow you to recognize the early signs of anxiety and proactively employ peace-inducing techniques.

4. Engage in activities that promote relaxation and well-being, such as spending time in nature, listening to calming music, or engaging in hobbies that bring you joy. These activities can help you cultivate a sense of inner peace that can be carried into all areas of your life.

The Shield Of Faith

Chapter Summary

Faith is presented as an impenetrable shield, protecting us from the attacks of doubt, unbelief, and spiritual deception.

Faith is defined as not merely an intellectual assent but as a deep-seated trust and unwavering belief in God and His promises. Faith is not a passive acceptance but an active engagement with God's revelation, enabling us to perceive spiritual realities and live according to God's truth.

The author highlights the importance of the shield of faith in spiritual warfare, emphasizing its power to quench the enemy's fiery darts, which represent doubt, unbelief, and spiritual deception. These darts are designed to undermine our faith, causing us to question God's character, His promises, and our ability to overcome challenges. The shield of faith provides a solid defense, deflecting these attacks and preserving our confidence in God.

She emphasizes the transformative power of faith, highlighting its ability to dispel doubt, strengthen resolve, and empower us to stand firm in the face of spiritual opposition. As we raise the shield of faith, we experience the assurance and protection that come from trusting in God's unwavering promises and His sovereign control over all things.

To effectively utilize the shield of faith, she suggests practical steps such as:

- Grounding your faith in the solid foundation of God's Word, diligently studying Scripture and seeking its guidance in all aspects of life. This provides a clear understanding of God's character, His promises, and His ways.

- Nurturing your faith through daily prayer and meditation, communing with God and seeking His wisdom and strength. Prayer allows you to connect with God, express your faith, and receive His guidance in times of uncertainty.

- Living a life aligned with your faith, demonstrating your belief through your actions and decisions. This involves embodying God's values, pursuing righteousness, and sharing your faith with others.

- Engaging in spiritual disciplines, such as fasting, confession, and submission to God's will. These practices strengthen your faith, deepen your relationship with God, and prepare you to face spiritual challenges.

Key Lessons

1. Faith is not merely intellectual assent but a deep-seated trust and unwavering belief in God and His promises. It is not a passive acceptance but an active engagement with God's revelation, enabling us to perceive spiritual realities and live according to God's truth.

2. The shield of faith is crucial in spiritual warfare, providing an impenetrable defense against the enemy's fiery darts of doubt, unbelief, and spiritual deception. These darts seek to undermine our faith, causing us to question God's character, His promises, and our ability to overcome challenges.

3. Faith is strengthened through a solid foundation in God's Word, daily prayer and meditation, living a life aligned with faith, and engaging in spiritual disciplines. These practices provide nourishment, assurance, and preparation for spiritual battles.

4. Standing firm in faith provides unwavering protection against the enemy's attacks. With faith as our shield, we can confidently face spiritual opposition, trusting in God's promises and His unwavering love and protection.

Self-reflection questions

How has your understanding of faith, as both a gift from God and a personal conviction, shaped your approach to spiritual warfare and your trust in God's promises?

_____

_____

_____

_____

_____

_____

_____

In what ways have you experienced the enemy's attempts to undermine your faith, introducing seeds of doubt, unbelief, or spiritual deception? How have you recognized and resisted these attacks?

_____

_____

_____

_____

_____

_____

_____

How can you cultivate a deeper commitment to grounding your faith in the solid foundation of God's Word, regularly studying Scripture and seeking its guidance in all aspects of your life?

_____

_____

_____

_____

_____

_____

_____

_____

How can you nurture your faith through daily prayer and meditation, actively engaging with God, expressing your faith, and seeking His wisdom and strength in times of uncertainty?

_____

_____

_____

_____

_____

_____

_____

_____

How can you align your actions with your faith, demonstrating your belief through your decisions, behaviors, and interactions with others?

_____

_____

_____

_____

_____

_____

_____

_____

How can you incorporate spiritual disciplines, such as fasting, confession, and submission to God's will, into your daily life? How do these practices strengthen your faith and prepare you for spiritual challenges?

_____

_____

_____

_____

_____

_____

_____

_____

_____

In what ways can you share your faith journey with others, providing encouragement, support, and a reflection of the transformative power of faith in your own life?

_____

_____

_____

_____

_____

_____

_____

_____

Life-Changing Exercises

1. Create a personalized "Faith Journal" where you regularly record moments of doubt or questioning and their corresponding responses from Scripture. This will help you identify patterns, recognize the enemy's tactics, and develop a library of God's promises to combat doubt.

2. Engage in regular memorization of key verses that speak to faith, trust, and overcoming challenges. This will allow you to quickly access God's Word in moments of doubt and uncertainty, reminding yourself of His promises and strengthening your resolve.

3. Practice active confession of unbelief and doubt, bringing these thoughts to God and seeking His forgiveness and renewed faith. This will cleanse your heart and mind, creating space for God's unwavering truth to take root.

4. Seek out opportunities to share your faith journey with trusted friends, mentors, or small group members. This will provide accountability, encouragement, and opportunities to learn from others' experiences, fostering a stronger and more resilient faith.

The Helmet Of Salvation

Chapter Summary

Salvation is presented as a secure covering, safeguarding our thoughts, beliefs, and understanding from the enemy's attempts to distort our perception of truth and undermine our spiritual well-being.

She begins by defining salvation as not merely a future event or a past decision but as a present reality that shapes our identity and provides ongoing protection from spiritual harm. Salvation is not about earning God's favor but about receiving His gift of redemption, becoming a new creation in Christ, and being reconciled to our Creator.

She then highlights the importance of the helmet of salvation in spiritual warfare, emphasizing its power to guard our minds, the seat of our thoughts, beliefs, and decision-making. The mind is a primary target of the enemy's attacks, as it is the source of our perceptions and the foundation of our actions. The helmet of salvation provides a secure covering, preventing the enemy from infiltrating our thoughts, planting seeds of doubt, and distorting our understanding of God's truth.

The author emphasizes the transformative power of salvation, highlighting its ability to renew our minds, transform our thoughts, and empower us to make wise decisions. As we put on the helmet of salvation, we experience the mind-renewing work of the Holy Spirit, who aligns our thoughts with God's perspective and grants us discernment to navigate the complexities of life.

To effectively utilize the helmet of salvation, the author suggests practical steps such as:

- Surrendering our minds to God's control, allowing Him to transform our thoughts and beliefs according to His truth. This involves actively engaging with Scripture, seeking God's guidance in decision-making, and guarding against thoughts that contradict God's revealed truth.

- Actively filling our minds with truth and positivity, engaging in activities that nourish our faith and strengthen our understanding of God's character. This includes reading Scripture, listening to uplifting music, and surrounding ourselves with positive and encouraging influences.

- Challenging negative and distorted thoughts, bringing them to the light of God's truth and refusing to let them take root in our minds. This involves practicing mindfulness, identifying toxic thoughts, and actively countering them with God's promises and affirmations.

- Praying for protection and clarity of mind, seeking God's guidance in navigating challenging thoughts and situations. This allows us to rely on God's wisdom and discernment in moments of uncertainty and resist the enemy's attempts to distort our perceptions.

Key Lessons

1. Salvation is not merely a future event or a past decision but a present reality that shapes our identity and provides ongoing protection from spiritual harm. It is a gift from God that redeems us, reconciles us to Him, and makes us new creations in Christ.

2. The helmet of salvation is crucial in spiritual warfare, guarding our minds, the seat of our thoughts, beliefs, and decision-making. It protects us from the enemy's attempts to infiltrate

our thoughts, plant seeds of doubt, and distort our understanding of God's truth.

3. Wearing the helmet of salvation involves surrendering our minds to God's control, allowing Him to transform our thoughts and beliefs according to His truth. It also involves actively filling our minds with truth and positivity, challenging negative thoughts, and praying for protection and clarity of mind.

4. Standing firm in faith and wearing the helmet of salvation provides assurance and protection against the enemy's attacks on our minds. It allows us to confidently engage with the world, knowing that our identity as God's beloved children is secure and our minds are guarded by His truth.

Self-reflection questions

How has your understanding of salvation, as both a gift from God and a transformative experience, shaped your approach to spiritual warfare and your perception of your identity as a child of God?

_____

_____

_____

_____

_____

_____

In what ways have you experienced the enemy's attempts to attack your mind, introducing thoughts of doubt, fear, or distorted perceptions of truth? How have you recognized and resisted these attacks?

_____

_____

_____

_____

_____

_____

_____

_____

How can you cultivate a deeper commitment to surrendering your mind to God's control, actively seeking His guidance in shaping your thoughts and beliefs according to His truth?

_____

_____

_____

_____

_____

_____

_____

How can you make a habit of filling your mind with truth and positivity, engaging in activities that nourish your faith, strengthen your understanding of God's character, and cultivate a hopeful and optimistic outlook?

_____

_____

_____

_____

_____

_____

_____

How can you effectively challenge negative and distorted thoughts that arise in your mind, bringing them to the light of God's truth and refusing to let them take root and influence your decisions?

_____

_____

_____

_____

_____

_____

_____

How can you incorporate regular prayer into your daily life, specifically seeking God's protection and clarity of mind, especially when facing challenging thoughts or situations that require discernment?

_____

_____

_____

_____

_____

_____

How can you share your experiences of spiritual warfare and the transformative power of salvation with others, providing encouragement, support, and a reflection of the ongoing protection that comes from wearing the helmet of salvation?

_____

_____

_____

_____

_____

_____

_____

Life-Changing Exercises

1. Establish a daily meditation practice, focusing on Scripture verses that speak to salvation, redemption, and the security of your identity as a child of God. This will help you internalize God's

truth, combat negative thoughts, and cultivate a sense of peace and confidence in your salvation.

2. Create a "Gratitude Journal" where you regularly record moments of God's provision, blessings, and evidence of His love and faithfulness. This will help you maintain a positive outlook, counter negativity, and cultivate a heart of appreciation that strengthens your faith and shields your mind from doubt.

3. Engage in creative expressions that reflect your faith and understanding of salvation, such as writing songs, journaling, painting, or crafting. This will allow you to process your spiritual experiences, deepen your connection to God, and share your faith journey with others in a meaningful way.

4. Seek out opportunities to mentor or encourage others who are struggling with doubt, fear, or distorted perceptions of truth. Share your own experiences of overcoming spiritual attacks and point them to God's Word for guidance and protection. By helping others, you will also strengthen your own faith and deepen your understanding of salvation's transformative power.

The Sword Of The Spirit

Chapter Summary

The sword of the Spirit is presented as the powerful Word of God, wielded by the Holy Spirit to combat the enemy's schemes and defend against his attacks.

The author defines the sword of the Spirit as not merely a physical text but as the living, active Word of God, inspired by the Holy Spirit and possessing the power to transform lives and overcome spiritual opposition. The Word of God is not a passive collection of words but a dynamic force that can penetrate hearts, reveal truth, and set captives free.

She highlights the importance of the sword of the Spirit in spiritual warfare, emphasizing its ability to cut through deception, expose lies, and defeat the enemy's strategies. The sword of the Spirit is not merely a defensive tool but an offensive weapon, capable of dismantling strongholds of sin, breaking chains of bondage, and gaining victory over spiritual adversaries.

There is emphasis on the transformative power of the sword of the Spirit, highlighting its ability to convict hearts, guide believers towards righteousness, and empower them to live according to God's will.

The Word of God is not just a weapon against the enemy but a tool for personal growth and spiritual transformation.

To effectively utilize the sword of the Spirit, the author suggests practical steps such as:

- Diligently studying Scripture, engaging with God's Word on a daily basis, and seeking to understand its application in all aspects of life. This will equip you with knowledge, wisdom, and discernment, allowing you to wield the sword of the Spirit with confidence and accuracy.

- Memorizing key verses that speak to spiritual warfare, truth, and victory over the enemy. This will provide you with readily available ammunition in moments of spiritual conflict, enabling you to stand firm on God's promises and resist the enemy's attacks.

- Applying the Word of God to your thoughts, actions, and decisions, allowing it to guide your choices and shape your character. This will not only protect you from spiritual harm but also contribute to your overall growth and sanctification.

- Praying for the Holy Spirit's guidance in understanding and applying Scripture, seeking His wisdom to wield the sword of the Spirit effectively. This will ensure that you are using God's Word in a way that aligns with His will and brings forth His intended outcomes.

Key Lessons

1. The sword of the Spirit is not merely a physical text but the living, active Word of God, inspired by the Holy Spirit and possessing the power to transform lives and overcome spiritual opposition. It is not a passive collection of words but a dynamic force that can penetrate hearts, reveal truth, and set captives free.

2. The sword of the Spirit is crucial in spiritual warfare, providing a powerful offensive weapon to cut through deception, expose lies, and defeat the enemy's strategies. It is not just a defensive tool but a means to dismantle strongholds of sin, break chains of bondage, and gain victory over spiritual adversaries.

3. Wielding the sword of the Spirit effectively involves diligently studying Scripture, memorizing key verses, applying the Word of

God to daily life, and praying for the Holy Spirit's guidance in understanding and applying Scripture. This equips us with knowledge, wisdom, discernment, and the ability to use God's Word in a way that aligns with His will.

4. Grasping the Word of God, empowered by the Holy Spirit, makes us formidable warriors in spiritual warfare, capable of defeating the enemy's schemes and standing firm in the face of opposition. With the sword of the Spirit in hand, we can confidently proclaim God's truth, expose deception, and live victorious lives in Christ.

Self-reflection questions

How has your understanding of the Word of God, as both a divine revelation and a powerful weapon, shaped your approach to spiritual warfare and your reliance on God's guidance?

_____

_____

_____

_____

In what ways have you experienced the enemy's attempts to distort your understanding of truth, sow seeds of doubt, or misrepresent God's character? How have you recognized and countered these attacks with the sword of the Spirit?

How can you cultivate a deeper commitment to diligent study of Scripture, engaging with God's Word on a regular basis, and seeking to understand its application in all aspects of life?

_____

_____

_____

_____

_____

_____

_____

How can you incorporate memorization of key verses into your daily routine, selecting passages that speak to truth, victory, and spiritual warfare? How can you use these verses as a shield against deception and a weapon against the enemy's schemes?

_____

_____

_____

_____

_____

_____

_____

_____

How can you actively apply the principles and teachings of Scripture to your thoughts, actions, and decisions, allowing God's Word to guide your choices and shape your character?

_____

_____

_____

_____

_____

_____

_____

_____

How can you incorporate regular prayer into your daily
life, specifically seeking the Holy Spirit's guidance in
understanding and applying Scripture, asking for
wisdom to wield the sword of the Spirit effectively?

_____

_____

_____

_____

_____

_____

How can you share your understanding of the sword of the Spirit and the power of God's Word with others, encouraging them to engage with Scripture, seek spiritual growth, and stand firm in the face of spiritual opposition?

Life-Changing Exercises

1. Create a "Scripture Memory Box" where you collect and organize verses that speak to truth, victory, and spiritual warfare. Regularly review these verses, incorporating them into your prayers, meditations, and daily conversations. This will help you internalize God's truth, strengthen your faith, and prepare yourself to wield the sword of the Spirit effectively.

2. Establish a daily "Sword Time" routine, dedicating specific time each day to studying, meditating on, and applying Scripture to your life. This could involve reading a chapter of the Bible, journaling your reflections, memorizing key verses, or seeking guidance from trusted spiritual mentors. This consistent engagement with God's Word will equip you with the knowledge, wisdom, and discernment needed to navigate spiritual battles with confidence.

3. Engage in creative expressions that reflect your understanding of the sword of the Spirit and the power of God's Word. This could involve writing songs, poems, or journal entries, creating artwork, or even developing a multimedia presentation. By creatively expressing your faith, you will deepen your own understanding, inspire

others, and contribute to a vibrant community of believers who value the sword of the Spirit.

4. Become a "Sword Carrier" for others, sharing your knowledge and experience in wielding the sword of the Spirit with those who are struggling with doubt, fear, or spiritual opposition. Offer to mentor, teach, or simply listen to others as they navigate their own spiritual journeys. By sharing the power of God's Word with others, you will not only strengthen their faith but also deepen your own understanding and grow in your own spiritual maturity.

Final Evaluation Questions

What did you learn from this workbook that you didn't know before?

_____

_____

_____

_____

_____

How has the information in this workbook impacted your understanding of the subject matter?

_____

_____

_____

_____

Can you identify any areas where you still feel uncertain or would like further clarification?

_____

_____

_____

_____

Describe any challenges you faced while completing the exercises in this workbook and how you overcame them.

_____

_____

_____

_____

How do you plan to apply the knowledge and skills you've gained from this workbook in your work or daily life?

_____

_____

_____

_____

_____

Are there any specific topics or concepts you would like to explore further after completing this workbook?

_____

_____

_____

_____

Overall, how would you rate your learning experience with this workbook on a scale of 1 to 10, with 10 being the highest? Please explain your rating.

_____

_____

Dear reader,

Thank you for choosing this workbook. Your engagement with the content is truly appreciated. As an author, I am committed to continuous improvement and providing valuable insights to my readers.

I kindly request a moment of your time to share your thoughts on the book. Your honest review will not only provide valuable feedback but also assist potential readers in making informed decisions.

Please consider addressing the following points in your review:

What resonated with you the most?
Were the questions and exercises helpful?
How would you describe the overall impact of the book on your understanding or perspective?
Were the chapter summaries effective in reinforcing key concepts?

Your input is instrumental in shaping future projects and ensuring that they meet the expectations of readers like you. Feel free to express your thoughts openly, as your feedback is genuinely valued.

Once again, thank you for your time and consideration. Your support means the world, and I am eager to hear your insights.

Best Regards,
Willow Reads Workbook Team.

Made in the USA
Middletown, DE
19 December 2024

67775606R00049